OFFICIAL SQA PAST PAPERS
WITH ANSWERS

D1439350

INTERMEDIATE 2

ENGLISH
2007-2011

2007 EXAM — page 3
Close Reading
Critical Essay

2008 EXAM — page 13
Close Reading
Critical Essay

2009 EXAM — page 23
Close Reading
Critical Essay

2010 EXAM — page 33
Close Reading
Critical Essay

2011 EXAM — page 43
Close Reading
Critical Essay

ANSWER SECTION — page 55

Publisher's Note

We are delighted to bring you the 2011 Past Papers and you will see that we have changed the format from previous editions. As part of our environmental awareness strategy, we have attempted to make these new editions as sustainable as possible.

To do this, we have printed on white paper and bound the answer sections into the book. This not only allows us to use significantly less paper but we are also, for the first time, able to source all the materials from sustainable sources.

We hope you like the new editions and by purchasing this product, you are not only supporting an independent Scottish publishing company but you are also, in the International Year of Forests, not contributing to the destruction of the world's forests.

Thank you for your support and please see the following websites for more information to support the above statement –

www.fsc-uk.org

www.loveforests.com

© Scottish Qualifications Authority
All rights reserved. Copying prohibited. No part of this publication may be reproduced, stored in a retrieval system, or transmitted in any form or by any means, electronic, mechanical, photocopying, recording or otherwise.

First exam published in 2007.
Published by Bright Red Publishing Ltd, 6 Stafford Street, Edinburgh EH3 7AU
tel: 0131 220 5804 fax: 0131 220 6710 info@brightredpublishing.co.uk www.brightredpublishing.co.uk

ISBN 978-1-84948-197-7

A CIP Catalogue record for this book is available from the British Library.

Bright Red Publishing is grateful to the copyright holders, as credited on the final page of the Question Section, for permission to use their material. Every effort has been made to trace the copyright holders and to obtain their permission for the use of copyright material. Bright Red Publishing will be happy to receive information allowing us to rectify any error or omission in future editions.

[BLANK PAGE]

X115/201

NATIONAL
QUALIFICATIONS
2007

FRIDAY, 11 MAY
1.00 PM – 2.00 PM

ENGLISH
INTERMEDIATE 2
Close Reading

Answer all questions.

30 marks are allocated to this paper.

Read the passage carefully and then answer **all** the questions, **using your own words as far as possible**.

The questions will ask you to show that:

you understand the main ideas and important details in the passage—in other words, **what** the writer has said (**Understanding–U**);

you can identify, using appropriate terms, the techniques the writer has used to get across these ideas—in other words, **how** he has said it (**Analysis–A**);

you can, using appropriate evidence, comment on how effective the writer has been—in other words, **how well** he has said it (**Evaluation–E**).

A code letter (U, A, E) is used alongside each question to identify its purpose for you. The number of marks attached to each question will give some indication of the length of answer required.

SCOTTISH
QUALIFICATIONS
AUTHORITY

©

Come fly with me

In this passage, the writer reflects on his fascination with birds and flight.

I was going through Monken Hadley churchyard and there were lots (note scientific precision) of house martins whizzing round the church tower. House martins are dapper little chaps, navy blue with white, and they are one of the sights of the summer: doing things like whizzing round church steeples and catching flies in their beaks. Later in the
5 season the young ones take up whizzing themselves, trying to get the hang of this flying business. So I paused on my journey to spend a few moments gazing at the whirligig of martins. It was nothing special, nothing exceptional, and it was very good indeed. Note this: one of the greatest pleasures of birdwatching is the quiet enjoyment of the absolutely ordinary.

10 And then it happened. Bam!

Gone.

From the tail of my eye, I saw what I took to be a kestrel. I turned my head to watch it as it climbed, and I waited for it to go into its hover, according to time-honoured kestrel custom. But it did nothing of the kind. It turned itself into an anchor. Or a
15 thunderbolt.

No kestrel this: it crashed into the crowd of martins, and almost as swiftly vanished. I think it got one, but I can't swear to it, it was all so fast.

It was a hobby-hawk. Perhaps the most dashing falcon of them all: slim, elegant and deadly fast. Not rare as rare-bird-addicts reckon things: they come to Britain in
20 reasonable numbers every summer to breed. The sight of a hobby-hawk makes no headlines in the birdwatching world. It was just a wonderful and wholly unexpected sight of a wonderful and wholly unexpected bird. It was a moment of perfect drama.

Birdwatching is a state of being, not an activity. It doesn't depend on place, on equipment, on specific purpose, like, say, fishing. It is not a matter of organic
25 trainspotting; it is about life and it is about living. It is a matter of keeping the eyes and ears and mind open. It is not a matter of obsession, not at all. It is just quiet enjoyment.

Flight is the dream of every human being. When we are lucky, we do, quite literally, dream about flying. They are the best of all dreams—you are free, you are miraculous.

The desire to fly is part of the condition of being human. That's why most of the
30 non-confrontational sports are about flying, or at least the defiance of gravity. Gymnastics is about the power of the human body to fly unaided; so is the high jump and the long jump. The throwing events—discus, shot-put and hammer—are about making something else fly: a war on gravity.

Golf always seems to me a trivial game, but every one of its legion of addicts will tell you
35 that it all comes back to the pure joy of a clean strike at the ball: making it defy gravity. Making it climb like a towering snipe. Making it soar like an eagle, at least in the mind of the striker, as it reaches the top of its long, graceful parabola.

Think about it: all these sports are done for the joy of flying. Skating is a victory over friction, and it feels like victory over gravity; it feels like flying. Its antithesis is
40 weightlifting: a huge and brutal event, the idea of which is to beat gravity. All the horsey events come back to the idea of flight: of getting off the ground, of escaping human limitations by joining up with another species and finding flight. For every rider, every horse has wings.

And birds fly in all kinds of ways: the brisk purpose of a sparrow, the airy detachment
45 of the seagull, the dramatic power of the hawk. Some birds specialise in flying very fast;
others in flying very slow. Great hunters such as the barn owl work on the edge of the
stall all the time. Kestrels are very good at flying without moving at all. Some birds are
not so great at flying. Pheasants just about get off the ground into a safe place in a tree
for a night. They are poor flyers, but they are unquestionably better than us humans.

50 And flight attracts our eyes, lifts our heart with joy and envy. Flight, to us earthbound
creatures, is a form of magic—one of the great powers attributed to decent wizards and
witches throughout history is the ability to fly, from the persecuted sorcerers of the Dark
Ages to the players of the game of quidditch.

Take a basic urban moment—a traffic jam, a train becalmed. A sigh, a look away from
55 the road or the newspaper, out of the window. A skein of geese in the sky; probably,
almost certainly, "just" Canada geese. Too far away to hear them honking to each other,
urgent instructions to keep the formation tight and to help the leader out with the hard
work. A daily sight, a common sight, an ordinary sight. But just for one
second—perhaps even two—you are let off the day's hassles. At least that is the case if
60 you take the trouble to look up. It will probably be the most inspiring thing you will see
all day. The day is the better for those birds.

And so we look to birds for a deep-seated kind of joy. It goes back to the dawn of
humankind: ever since humans first walked upright, they were able to turn their eyes to
the heavens and observe the birds. The birds have something we can never have. But
65 merely by existing—by flying before us—they add to the daily joys of existence. Birds
are about hope.

Adapted from *How to be a Bad Birdwatcher* by Simon Barnes

QUESTIONS   *Marks Code*

1. Explain what is odd or ironic about the expression "note scientific precision" (lines 1–2).   2   A

2. "It was nothing special, nothing exceptional, and it was very good indeed." (line 7).

   (a) What is surprising about this statement?   1   A

   (b) Show how the writer continues this idea in the next sentence (lines 8–9).   2   U/A

3. Identify **two** techniques used in lines 10 and 11 which help to convey the idea of speed described in the next two paragraphs (lines 12–17).   2   A

4. (a) What is the author suggesting about the bird when he says "It turned itself into an anchor" (line 14)?   1   U/A

   (b) Why is the comparison of the bird to a "thunderbolt" (line 15) an effective image or metaphor?   2   E

5. Explain with clear reference to the whole sentence why the writer uses a colon in line 19.   2   A

6. "The sight of a hobby-hawk makes no headlines in the birdwatching world" (lines 20–21). Explain **in your own words** what is meant by "makes no headlines".   1   U

7. Write down the word from later in the paragraph which continues the idea introduced by "trainspotting" (line 25).   1   U

8. In what way does the author's use of "quite literally" (line 27) help to make his meaning clear?   1   U/A

9. (a) What does "trivial" (line 34) tell us about the writer's attitude to golf?   1   U

   (b) Explain how an expression later in this sentence makes it clear that the author is aware that others do not share his opinion.   2   U/A

   (c) Why are the comparisons the writer uses in the rest of this paragraph appropriate?   2   A/E

10. The writer mentions a variety of sports between lines 29 and 43. What challenge does he think these activities have in common?   1   U

11. The writer refers to equestrianism ("horsey events", line 41), as related to the pursuit of flight. What is the difference between this and all the other sports he mentions? Answer **in your own words**.   1   U

12. Why is it appropriate to introduce the paragraph consisting of lines 44 to 49 with the expression "And birds fly in all kinds of ways"?   2   A/E

13. The writer refers to "wizards and witches throughout history" (lines 51–52). Explain by referring to either **word choice** or **structure** how the rest of the sentence continues this idea.   2   U/A

14. What do the writer's examples of "a basic urban moment" (line 54) have in common?   1   U

15. What is the effect of the inverted commas round "just" in line 56?   1   A

16. Explain fully why the last paragraph (lines 62–66) provides an appropriate or effective conclusion to the passage.   2   E

[END OF QUESTION PAPER]   **Total (30)**

X115/202

| NATIONAL QUALIFICATIONS 2007 | FRIDAY, 11 MAY 2.20 PM – 3.50 PM | ENGLISH INTERMEDIATE 2 Critical Essay |

Answer **two** questions.

Each question must be taken from a different section.

Each question is worth 25 marks.

SCOTTISH
QUALIFICATIONS
AUTHORITY

©

Answer TWO questions from this paper.

Each question must be chosen from a different Section (A–E). You are not allowed to choose two questions from the same Section.

In all Sections you may use Scottish texts.

Write the number of each question in the margin of your answer booklet and begin each essay on a fresh page.

You should spend about 45 minutes on each essay.

The following will be assessed:

- the relevance of your essays to the questions you have chosen

- your knowledge and understanding of key elements, central concerns and significant details of the chosen texts

- your explanation of ways in which aspects of structure/style/language contribute to the meaning/effect/impact of the chosen texts

- your evaluation of the effectiveness of the chosen texts, supported by detailed and relevant evidence

- the quality and technical accuracy of your writing.

Each question is worth 25 marks. The total for this paper is 50 marks.

SECTION A—DRAMA

Answers to questions in this section should refer to the text and to such relevant features as: characterisation, key scene(s), structure, climax, theme, plot, conflict, setting . . .

1. Choose a play which portrays a strong relationship between two of the main characters.

    Describe the nature of the relationship and explain how the relationship influences the fate of the two characters concerned.

2. Choose a play in which there is a highly emotional scene.

    Show how this scene increases your understanding of the characters involved and how it is important in the unfolding of the plot of the play.

3. Choose a play which has, as a central concern, an issue which is of importance in today's society.

    State what the issue is and show how the playwright's handling of the plot and characters increases your understanding of the issue.

SECTION B—PROSE

Answers to questions in this section should refer to the text and to such relevant features as: characterisation, setting, language, key incident(s), climax/turning point, plot, structure, narrative technique, theme, ideas, description . . .

4. Choose a novel **or** short story in which **two** of the main characters have a disagreement which is important to the outcome of the novel or short story.

   Identify the reasons for the disagreement and go on to show how the effects of the disagreement have an impact on the rest of the novel or short story.

5. Choose a prose text (fiction or non-fiction) in which a society **or** a person **or** a culture **or** a setting is effectively portrayed.

   Show how the writer's presentation of the subject makes an impact on you, and helps you to understand the subject in greater depth.

6. Choose a novel **or** short story which has a striking opening.

   Show how the opening is effective in introducing the character(s) **and/or** the atmosphere **and/or** the setting.

SECTION C—POETRY

Answers to questions in this section should refer to the text and to such relevant features as: word choice, tone, imagery, structure, content, rhythm, theme, sound, ideas . . .

7. Choose a poem which seems to be about an ordinary everyday experience but which actually makes a deeper comment about life.

   Explain what the poem is about and go on to show how the techniques used by the poet help to make the ideas memorable.

8. Choose a poem which creates pity or sympathy in you.

   Show how the feelings of pity or sympathy are brought into focus by the use of poetic techniques.

9. Choose a poem which describes a scene or incident vividly.

   Briefly state what is being described and then go on to show how the poetic techniques used make the description vivid.

[Turn over

SECTION D—FILM AND TV DRAMA

Answers to questions in this section should refer to the text and to such relevant features as: use of camera, key sequence, characterisation, mise-en-scène, editing, setting, music/sound effects, plot, dialogue . . .

10. Choose a film or TV drama* which creates suspense or tension either in a particular scene **or** throughout the whole film or TV drama.

    Show how the suspense or tension is created and how it affects your enjoyment of the film or TV drama* as a whole.

11. Choose a film or TV drama* which deals with crime **or** espionage **or** detection.

    Show how the film or TV drama* captures and holds your interest by its choice of content and use of media techniques.

12. Choose a film or TV drama* which depends to some extent on humour to make an impact.

    Briefly state what you consider to be the humorous aspects of the film or TV drama* and go on to show how the film or programme makers use various techniques to create the humour.

    * "TV drama" includes a single play, a series or a serial.

SECTION E—LANGUAGE

Answers to questions in this section should refer to the text and to such relevant features as: register, accent, dialect, slang, jargon, vocabulary, tone, abbreviation . . .

13. Consider the aspects of language which make advertising effective.

    Choose two advertisements which you feel vary in their effectiveness. By looking closely at each advertisement explain why you felt that one was more effective than the other.

14. Consider the language of two groups of people who are different in some significant way. For example, they may be from different generations or different places.

    By looking at examples of the language of each group, describe the differences between the two, and discuss the advantages **and/or** disadvantages which might arise from the different ways of using language.

15. Consider a modern means of communication such as e-mailing or text-messaging.

    By referring to specific examples show what are the advantages and disadvantages of the method of communication which you have chosen.

[END OF QUESTION PAPER]

2008

[BLANK PAGE]

X115/201

NATIONAL
QUALIFICATIONS
2008

THURSDAY, 15 MAY
1.00 PM – 2.00 PM

ENGLISH
INTERMEDIATE 2
Close Reading

Answer all questions.

30 marks are allocated to this paper.

Read the passage carefully and then answer **all** the questions, **using your own words as far as possible**.

The questions will ask you to show that:

you understand the main ideas and important details in the passage—in other words, **what** the writer has said (**Understanding–U**);

you can identify, using appropriate terms, the techniques the writer has used to get across these ideas—in other words, **how** he has said it (**Analysis–A**);

you can, using appropriate evidence, comment on how effective the writer has been—in other words, **how well** he has said it (**Evaluation–E**).

A code letter (U, A, E) is used alongside each question to identify its purpose for you. The number of marks attached to each question will give some indication of the length of answer required.

Afar, far away

Matthew Parris describes the harsh conditions of life in North Africa, and suggests what may be in store for the region and the nomadic (wandering) people who live there.

At the beginning of this month I was in a hellish yet beautiful place. I was making a programme for Radio 4 about one of the world's most ancient trade routes. Every year, since (we suppose) at least the time of the Ancient Greeks, hundreds of thousands of camels are led, strung together in trains, from the highlands of Ethiopia into the Danakil
5 depression: a descent into the desert of nearly 10,000 feet, a journey of about 100 miles. Here, by the edge of a blue-black and bitter salt lake, great floes of rock salt encrusting the mud are prised up, hacked into slabs and loaded on to the camels.

Then the camels and their drivers make the climb through dry mountains back into the highlands, where the slabs are bound with tape and distributed across the Horn of
10 Africa. The camels drink only twice on their journey, walking often at night, and carrying with them straw to eat on the way back. Their drivers bring only dry bread, sugar and tea.

Travelling with the camel trains in mid-winter, when temperatures are bearable, I found the experience extraordinarily moving. But my thoughts went beyond the salt trade, and
15 were powerfully reinforced by the journey that followed it—to another desert, the Algerian Sahara.

These reflections were first prompted by a chance remark that could not have been more wrong. Our superb Ethiopian guide, Solomon Berhe, was sitting with me in a friendly but flyblown village of sticks, stones, cardboard and tin in Hamed Ela, 300ft below sea
20 level, in a hot wind, on a hot night. An infinity of stars blazed above. The mysterious lake was close, and when the wind changed you could smell the sulphur blowing from a range of bubbling vents of gas, salt and super-heated steam. On the horizon fumed the volcano, Hertale. With not a blade of grass in sight, and all around us a desert of black rocks, the Danakil is a kind of inferno. How the Afar people manage to live in
25 this place, and why they choose to, puzzles the rest of Ethiopia, as it does me.

"But," said Solomon, scratching one of the small fly-bites that were troubling all of us, "if we could return here in 50 years, this village would be different. There will be streets, electricity, and proper buildings. As Ethiopia modernises, places like this will be made more comfortable for people. Hamed Ela will probably be a big town."

30 And that is where Solomon was wrong. As Ethiopia modernises, the Afar will leave their desert home. They will drift into the towns and cities in the highlands. Their voracious herds of goats will die. Their camels will no longer be of any use. The only remembrance this place will have of the humans it bred will be the stone fittings of their flimsy, ruined stick huts, and the mysterious black rock burial mounds that litter the
35 landscape.

There is no modern reason for human beings to live in such places. Their produce is pitiful, the climate brutal and the distances immense. Salt is already produced as cheaply by industrial means. If market forces don't kill the trade, the conscience of the animal rights movement will, for the laden camels suffer horribly on their journey. The
40 day is coming when camels will go down there no more. In fifty years the Danakil will be a national park, visited by rubbernecking tourists in helicopters. Camels will be found in zoos. Goats will be on their way to elimination from every ecologically fragile part of the planet.

Even in America, deserts are not properly inhabited any more. Unreal places such as
45 Las Vegas have sprung up where people live in an air-conditioned and artificially
irrigated bubble, but the land itself is emptier than before. Tribes who were part of the
land, and lived off it, have mostly gone, their descendants living in reservations. The
wilderness places of North America are vast and exceptionally well preserved; but they
are not part of many people's lives, except those of tourists. We are becoming outsiders
50 to the natural world, watching it on the Discovery Channel.

Those who call themselves environmentalists celebrate this. "Leave nothing and take
nothing away," read the signs at the gates of nature reserves. Practical advice, perhaps,
but is there not something melancholy in what that says about modern man's desired
relationship with nature? Will we one day confine ourselves to watching large parts of
55 our planet only from observation towers?

I have no argument against the international development movement that wants to see
the Afars in clean houses with running water and electrical power, and schools, and a
clinic nearby—away, in other words, from their gruesome desert life. All this is
inevitable.

60 But as that new way of living arrives—as we retreat from the wild places, and the fences
of national parks go up; as we cease the exploitation of animals, and the cow, the camel,
the sheep, the chicken and the pig become items in modern exhibition farms, where
schoolchildren see how mankind used to live; as our direct contact with our fellow
creatures is restricted to zoos, pets and fish tanks; and as every area of natural beauty is
65 set about with preservation orders and rules to keep human interference to a
minimum—will we not be separating ourselves from our planet in order, as we suppose,
to look after it better? Will we not be loving nature, but leaving it?

They say there is less traffic across the Sahara today than at any time in human history,
even if you include motor transport. The great days of camel caravans are over. As for
70 the inhabitants, the nomads are on a path to extinction as a culture. Nomadic life does
not fit the pattern of nation states, taxes, frontiers and controls. And though for them
there is now government encouragement to stay, their culture is doomed. Amid the
indescribable majesty of this place—the crumbling towers of black rock, the scream of
the jackal, the waterless canyons, yellow dunes, grey plateaus and purple thorn
75 bushes—I have felt like a visitor to a monumental ruin, walked by ghosts. There are
fragments of pottery, thousands of cave paintings of deer, giraffe, elephant, and men in
feathers, dancing . . . but no people, not a soul.

In the beginning, man is expelled from the Garden of Eden. In the end, perhaps, we
shall leave it of our own accord, closing the gate behind us.

From *The Times,* February 25, 2006 (slightly adapted)

QUESTIONS

Marks Cod

1. What is surprising about the writer's **word choice** in the first sentence? — 2 A

2. Why does the writer add the expression "we suppose" (line 3) to the sentence here? — 1 U

3. The word "floes" (line 6) usually refers to icebergs.

   Explain how it is appropriate to use it as a metaphor to refer to the appearance of the rock salt deposits. — 2 A/E

4. Explain how any **one** example of the writer's choice of descriptive detail in lines 10–12 emphasises the hardships of the journey. — 1 A

5. Explain **in your own words** the contrasting impressions the writer has of the village in Hamed Ela (see lines 18–19). — 2 U

6. Explain what the word "fumed" (line 22) suggests about the volcano, apart from having smoke coming from it. — 1 U

7. Explain why the sentence "And that is where Solomon was wrong" (line 30) is an effective link between the paragraphs contained in lines 26 to 35. — 2 E

8. What does the word "drift" suggest about how "the Afar will leave their desert home" (lines 30 –31)? — 1 U

9. The writer tells us "There is no modern reason for human beings to live in such places" (line 36).

   Explain **in your own words two** reasons why this is the case.

   Look in the next three sentences (lines 36–39) for your answer. — 2 U

10. Explain fully the appropriateness of the **word choice** of "rubbernecking tourists in helicopters" (line 41). — 2 A

11. Explain how the writer develops the idea of Las Vegas being "Unreal" (line 44). — 2 A

12. Explain why the expression "watching it on the Discovery Channel" (line 50) effectively illustrates our relationship with "wilderness places". — 2 E

13. What is the effect of the writer's inclusion of the words "Those who call themselves" in the sentence beginning in line 51? — 1 U

14. What is the **tone** of the two sentences in lines 52–55? — 1 A

15. Explain how other words in lines 56–58 help us to work out the meaning or sense of "gruesome desert life". — 2 U

16. Look at lines 60–67.

    (*a*) Identify any feature of **sentence structure** the writer uses effectively in this paragraph. — 1 A

    (*b*) Show how your chosen feature helps to clarify or support the writer's argument. — 2 A

17. Explain **in your own words** why "the nomads are on a path to extinction as a culture" (line 70). — 1 U

18. Explain any reason why the final paragraph (lines 78–79) works well as a conclusion to the passage. — 2 E

Total (30)

[END OF QUESTION PAPER]

X115/202

NATIONAL
QUALIFICATIONS
2008

THURSDAY, 15 MAY
2.20 PM – 3.50 PM

ENGLISH
INTERMEDIATE 2
Critical Essay

Answer **two** questions.

Each question must be taken from a different section.

Each question is worth 25 marks.

Answer TWO questions from this paper.

Each question must be chosen from a different Section (A–E). You are not allowed to choose two questions from the same Section.

In all Sections you may use Scottish texts.

Write the number of each question in the margin of your answer booklet and begin each essay on a fresh page.

You should spend about 45 minutes on each essay.

The following will be assessed:

- the relevance of your essays to the questions you have chosen

- your knowledge and understanding of key elements, central concerns and significant details of the chosen texts

- your explanation of ways in which aspects of structure/style/language contribute to the meaning/effect/impact of the chosen texts

- your evaluation of the effectiveness of the chosen texts, supported by detailed and relevant evidence

- the quality and technical accuracy of your writing.

Each question is worth 25 marks. The total for this paper is 50 marks.

SECTION A—DRAMA

Answers to questions in this section should refer to the text and to such relevant features as: characterisation, key scene(s), structure, climax, theme, plot, conflict, setting . . .

1. Choose a play in which there is a significant conflict between two characters.

   Describe the conflict and show how it is important to the development of the characterisation and theme of the play.

2. Choose a play which has a tragic ending.

   Show how the ending of the play results from the strengths and/or weaknesses of the main character(s).

3. Choose a play in which a character encounters difficulties within the community in which he or she lives.

   Show how the character copes with the difficulties he or she encounters and how his or her actions contribute to the theme of the play.

SECTION B—PROSE

Answers to questions in this section should refer to the text and to such relevant features as: characterisation, setting, language, key incident(s), climax/turning point, plot, structure, narrative technique, theme, ideas, description . . .

4. Choose a novel **or** short story which has a turning point or moment of realisation for at least one of the characters.

   Briefly describe what has led up to the turning point or moment. Go on to show what impact this has on the character(s) and how it affects the outcome of the novel or story.

5. Choose a novel **or** short story in which you feel sympathy with one of the main characters because of the difficulties or injustice or hardships she or he has to face.

   Describe the problems the character faces and show by what means you are made to feel sympathy for her or him.

6. Choose a non-fiction text **or** group of texts which uses setting, **or** humour, **or** description to make clear to you an interesting aspect of a society.

   Show how the use of any of these techniques helped you to understand the writer's point of view on the interesting aspect of this society.

SECTION C—POETRY

Answers to questions in this section should refer to the text and to such relevant features as: word choice, tone, imagery, structure, content, rhythm, theme, sound, ideas . . .

7. Choose a poem which creates an atmosphere of sadness, pity, or loss.

   Show how the poet creates the atmosphere and what effect it has on your response to the subject matter of the poem.

8. Choose a poem about a strong relationship—for example, between two people, or between a person and a place.

   Show how the poet, by the choice of content and the skilful use of techniques, helps you to appreciate the strength of the relationship.

9. Choose a poem which reflects on an aspect of human behaviour in such a way as to deepen your understanding of human nature.

   Describe the aspect of human behaviour which you have identified and show how the poet's use of ideas and techniques brought you to a deeper understanding of human nature.

[Turn over

SECTION D—FILM AND TV DRAMA

Answers to questions in this section should refer to the text and to such relevant features as: use of camera, key sequence, characterisation, mise-en-scène, editing, setting, music/sound effects, plot, dialogue . . .

10. Choose a film or TV drama* which involves the pursuit of power or the fulfilment of an ambition.

    Show how the theme is developed through the presentation of character and setting.

11. Choose an opening sequence from a film which effectively holds your interest and makes you want to watch the rest of the film.

    Show what elements of the opening sequence have this effect, and how they relate to the film as a whole.

12. Choose a film or TV drama* which reflects an important aspect of society.

    Describe the aspect of society being dealt with and show how the techniques used by the film or programme maker help to deepen your understanding of the importance of this aspect.

* "TV drama" includes a single play, a series or a serial.

SECTION E—LANGUAGE

Answers to questions in this section should refer to the text and to such relevant features as: register, accent, dialect, slang, jargon, vocabulary, tone, abbreviation . . .

13. Consider the language of advertising.

    In any one advertisement identify the ways in which language is used successfully. Explain what it is about these usages which makes them effective.

14. Consider the language of any form of modern electronic communication.

    Identify some features of this language which differ from normal usage and say how effective you think these features are in communicating information.

15. Consider the distinctive language of any specific group of people.

    What aspects of the group's language are distinctive and what advantage does the group gain from the use of such language?

[END OF QUESTION PAPER]

X115/202

NATIONAL
QUALIFICATIONS
2010

THURSDAY, 13 MAY
2.20 PM – 3.50 PM

ENGLISH
INTERMEDIATE 2
Critical Essay

Answer **two** questions.

Each question must be taken from a different section.

Each question is worth 25 marks.

Answer TWO questions from this paper.

Each question must be chosen from a different Section (A–E). You are not allowed to choose two questions from the same Section.

In all Sections you may use Scottish texts.

Write the number of each question in the margin of your answer booklet and begin each essay on a fresh page.

You should spend about 45 minutes on each essay.

The following will be assessed:

* **the relevance of your essays to the questions you have chosen**

* **your knowledge and understanding of key elements, central concerns and significant details of the chosen texts**

* **your explanation of ways in which aspects of structure/style/language contribute to the meaning/effect/impact of the chosen texts**

* **your evaluation of the effectiveness of the chosen texts, supported by detailed and relevant evidence**

* **the quality and technical accuracy of your writing.**

Each question is worth 25 marks. The total for this paper is 50 marks.

SECTION A—DRAMA

Answers to questions in this section should refer to the text and to such relevant features as: characterisation, key scene(s), structure, climax, theme, plot, conflict, setting . . .

1. Choose a play in which a central character feels increasingly isolated from those around her or him.

   Explain why the character finds herself or himself isolated, and show what the consequences are for the character concerned.

2. Choose a scene from a play in which there is an important incident which leads to a turning point in the action.

   Explain what happens in the scene, and then go on to say how it affects the outcome of the play.

3. Choose a play in which one of the main concerns is love **or** jealousy **or** betrayal **or** reconciliation.

   Explain what the concern is, and show how it is explored throughout the play.

SECTION B—PROSE

Answers to questions in this section should refer to the text and to such relevant features as: characterisation, setting, language, key incident(s), climax, turning point, plot, structure, narrative technique, theme, ideas, description . . .

4. Choose a novel **or** a short story which gives you an insight into an aspect of human nature or behaviour.

   State what the aspect is, and show how the characters' actions and relationships lead you to a deeper understanding of human nature or behaviour.

5. Choose a novel **or** a short story with an ending which you find satisfactory.

   By looking at the novel or short story as a whole, explain why you find the ending satisfactory in bringing to a conclusion the main concerns of the text.

6. Choose a prose work (fiction **or** non-fiction) in which setting is an important feature.

   Explain how the writer creates the setting, and then go on to show how this feature contributes to your understanding of the text as a whole.

SECTION C—POETRY

Answers to questions in this section should refer to the text and to such relevant features as: word choice, tone, imagery, structure, content, rhythm, theme, sound, ideas . . .

7. Choose a poem which could be considered as having a powerful message.

   Show how the poet effectively conveys this message through his or her use of poetic techniques.

8. Choose a poem in which the poet creates a particular mood or atmosphere.

   Show how the poet creates this mood or atmosphere by his or her choice of subject matter and use of poetic techniques.

9. Choose a poem which portrays an interesting character.

   Show how the poet uses poetic techniques to make the character interesting.

[Turn over

SECTION D—FILM AND TV DRAMA

> *Answers to questions in this section should refer to the text and to such relevant features as: use of camera, key sequence, characterisation, mise-en-scène, editing, setting, music/sound, special effects, plot, dialogue . . .*

10. Choose a film **or** TV drama* which deals with issues which mainly affect young people.

    Explain how the film or TV drama* deals with such issues, stating whether or not you find the portrayal of these issues realistic.

11. Choose a scene or sequence from a film or TV drama* which provides a climax to the action.

    Briefly describe the events leading up to the climax, and then explain how the techniques used by the film or programme makers create a heightened sense of importance in this scene or sequence.

12. Choose a film which you think is typical of its genre, for example: action, romance, comedy, horror . . .

    Explain how the film makers have used the features of the genre to create a successful film.

    * "TV drama" includes a single play, a series or a serial.

SECTION E—LANGUAGE

> *Answers to questions in this section should refer to the text and to such relevant features as: register, accent, dialect, slang, jargon, vocabulary, tone, abbreviation . . .*

13. Consider a text which you find to be persuasive, for example: an advertisement, a speech, a newspaper article . . .

    By referring to specific examples from your chosen text, show how persuasive techniques have been used to convince you.

14. Consider the ways that young people use the internet to communicate and socialise, for example: networking sites, instant messaging, chat rooms, blogs . . .

    By referring to specific examples of language and vocabulary, explain how such communication differs from formal English, and what its attractions are for young people.

15. Consider the specialist language used by any group which has a common leisure, vocational or geographical connection.

    Show how the specialist language used by the group is effective in communicating shared interests accurately.

[END OF QUESTION PAPER]

X270/202

NATIONAL
QUALIFICATIONS
2011

FRIDAY, 13 MAY
2.20 PM – 3.50 PM

ENGLISH
INTERMEDIATE 2
Critical Essay

Answer **two** questions.

Each question must be taken from a different section.

Each question is worth 25 marks.

Answer TWO questions from this paper.

Each question must be chosen from a different Section (A–E). You are not allowed to choose two questions from the same Section.

In all Sections you may use Scottish texts.

Write the number of each question in the margin of your answer booklet and begin each essay on a fresh page.

You should spend about 45 minutes on each essay.

The following will be assessed:

* the relevance of your essays to the questions you have chosen

* your knowledge and understanding of key elements, central concerns and significant details of the chosen texts

* your explanation of ways in which aspects of structure/style/language contribute to the meaning/effect/impact of the chosen texts

* your evaluation of the effectiveness of the chosen texts, supported by detailed and relevant evidence

* the quality and technical accuracy of your writing.

Each question is worth 25 marks. The total for this paper is 50 marks.

SECTION A—DRAMA

Answers to questions in this section should refer to the text and to such relevant features as: characterisation, key scene(s), structure, climax, theme, plot, conflict, setting . . .

1. Choose a play in which there is a character who suffers from a human weakness such as ambition, selfishness, lack of self-knowledge, jealousy, pride, lust . . .

    Show how the weakness is revealed, then explain how this weakness affects both the characters and the events of the play.

2. Choose a play in which there is an important relationship between two of the main characters.

    Describe the nature of the relationship, and explain how it is developed throughout the play.

3. Choose a play which you feel has a dramatic final scene.

    Describe briefly what happens and explain how effective the ending is in bringing to a conclusion the central concerns of the text.

SECTION B—PROSE

> *Answers to questions in this section should refer to the text and to such relevant features as: characterisation, setting, language, key incident(s), climax, turning point, plot, structure, narrative technique, theme, ideas, description . . .*

4. Choose a novel **or** a short story in which you feel there is an incident of great importance to the story as a whole.

   Describe the incident and go on to show its importance to the development of the characters and the central concerns of the text.

5. Choose a novel **or** a short story which has a character who affects you emotionally.

   Describe how you feel about the character, and show how the writer leads you to feel this way.

6. Choose a prose work (fiction **or** non-fiction) in which the writer uses a memorable style/voice/narrative technique.

   Explain in detail how features of the writing style/voice/narrative technique contribute to the effectiveness of the text.

SECTION C—POETRY

> *Answers to questions in this section should refer to the text and to such relevant features as: word choice, tone, imagery, structure, content, rhythm, theme, sound, ideas . . .*

7. Choose a poem which deals with an important issue such as war, crime, poverty **or** racism.

   Explain how the poet deepens your understanding of the issue by the choice of content and the skilful use of poetic techniques.

8. Choose a poem which describes an animal **or** a place **or** an event in an effective way.

   Briefly state what is being described and go on to show how the techniques used in the poem make the description effective.

9. Choose a poem written in a specific form such as ballad, sonnet, elegy, monologue, ode . . .

   Explain how the distinctive features of this form contribute to your appreciation of the text.

[Turn over

SECTION D—FILM AND TV DRAMA

> *Answers to questions in this section should refer to the text and to such relevant features as: use of camera, key sequence, characterisation, mise-en-scène, editing, setting, music/sound, special effects, plot, dialogue . . .*

10. Choose a film **or** TV drama* which has a character who could be described as a hero or as a villain.

    Explain how the the character is introduced and then developed throughout the film or TV drama.

11. Choose a film **or** TV drama* in which setting is an important feature.

    Explain how the setting is established and go on to show how the setting contributes to the effectiveness of the film **or** TV drama as a whole.

12. Choose a scene or sequence from a film **or** TV drama* in which an atmosphere of mystery, **or** horror, **or** suspense is created.

    Describe what happens in the scene or sequence, explaining how the techniques used by the film or programme makers create this atmosphere.

*   "TV drama" includes a single play, a series or a serial.

SECTION E—LANGUAGE

> *Answers to questions in this section should refer to the text and to such relevant features as: register, accent, dialect, slang, jargon, vocabulary, tone, abbreviation . . .*

13. Consider a text which aims to persuade people to support a particular group, **or** to buy a particular product.

    By referring to specific examples from your chosen text, show how persuasive techniques are used.

14. Consider a modern form of communication such as e-mail **or** text message.

    By referring to specific examples of language and vocabulary, explain how such communication differs from formal English, and what advantages this presents to users.

15. Consider the specialist language used by any group of people to talk about a particular interest, for example, a sport, a job, a hobby . . .

    By referring to specific examples, show how the specialist language used by the group is effective in communicating ideas clearly.

[END OF QUESTION PAPER]

[BLANK PAGE]

Acknowledgements

Permission has been sought from all relevant copyright holders and Bright Red Publishing is grateful for the use of the following:

An extract from 'How to be a Bad Birdwatcher' by Simon Barnes. Published by Short Books Ltd. (2007 Close Reading pages 2–3);

The article 'We are outsiders to the natural world, preferring to watch it on Discovery' taken from The Times, 25 February 2006. Reproduced by permission of Matthew Parris (2008 Close Reading pages 2–3);

An extract from 'A Child Called Freedom' by Carol Lee, published by Century 2006. Reprinted by permission of The Random House Group Ltd. (2009 Close Reading pages 2–3);

An extract from the article 'China's Colossus' by Damian Whitworth taken from The Times © The Times/NI Syndication August 30th 2007 (2010 Close Reading pages 2–3);

An extract from the article '2b or not 2b' by David Crystal from The Guardian, 5 June 2008. Originally from 'txtng: the gr8 db8' published by Oxford University Press, 2008 © David Crystal (2011 Close Reading pages 2–3).

INTERMEDIATE 2 | ANSWER SECTION

8. It conveys the hardship/protractedness/drudgery of the work

9. (a) It represents/stands for/is (readily) recognisable as representative (of China)

(b)

Gloss of "historical" or "age-old"	eg long-standing
Gloss of "separateness"	eg isolation
Gloss of "industriousness"	eg capacity for hard work

10. "establishing complete control over his empire" refers back to preceding ideas (relating to dominance)
"was not enough" prepares us for upcoming reference (to other things he wanted to do or have)
"But" introduces contrast

11. *Any two points from:*
He uses "may"; twice; he uses "some archaeologists" he uses "hope"; he uses "one day"; he uses "some form"

12.

Content	He refers to the large number of people involved in its construction OR the large number of pits OR the large number of artefacts found OR the possibility of many more OR the desire to have many servants etc. (paraphrase of last sentence) Generalised comment about large numbers acceptable
Technique	
Typography	he uses numerals (for impact)
Word choice	he uses "empire", which suggests size of construction OR he uses "army", which alludes to the large numbers of figures

One answer from each section needed for 2 marks

13.

word choice	"I can't think of anyone else"	(emphatically) conveys sense of uniqueness
	"scale of ambition"	(clearly) conveys size of imagination/ grandeur of plan
	"entire kingdom"	(clearly) conveys size of undertaking
	"Nobody else (in human history has attempted to do that)"	(emphatically) conveys sense of uniqueness/rareness
	"fascinating"	(clearly) suggests the captivating nature of (this aspect of) the story
structure	repetition of "anyone/ nobody else"	(clearly) emphasises uniqueness
	repetition of "we have no"	(clearly) emphasises uniqueness

One mark for feature, one for evaluative comment

14. Unusual/unconventional/strange/ironic/quaint/ peculiar

15. *Any one example and explanation from:*

"mass ranks"	recapitulates idea of large numbers
"Terracotta Army"	returns to an expression used in opening paragraph
"(breathtaking) megalomania"	recapitulates ideas/word used earlier
"wonders of the world"	recapitulates idea of magnificence
"(The telling of that story is long) overdue"	recapitulates idea of undeserved anonymity

ENGLISH INTERMEDIATE 2 CRITICAL ESSAY 2010

Please see Critical Essay Marking Principles on pages 64–65.

ENGLISH INTERMEDIATE 2
CLOSE READING
2011

1. (*a*) Any of "vandals", "(what) Genghis Khan (did to his neighbours)", "destroying", "pillaging", "savaging"

(*b*) Idea of alliteration
or similarity / balance of construction
e.g. both three-word phrases, both participial phrases, both containing "our"
or
identification of (humorous effect of) hyperbole

2.

textese	suffix "–ese" is pejorative
slanguage	(portmanteau) inclusion of "slang" is denigratory
virus	(metaphor) suggests destructiveness / disease / being harmful or unwanted
bleak	suggests (e.g.) poverty of language
bald	suggests (e.g.) plainness of language
sad	suggests regret about development or (more colloquial sense of) inadequacy
drab	suggests (e.g.) dreariness / monotony of language
shrinktalk	suggests impoverishment or (Orwellian) connotation of "-talk" suffix
masks	suggests (unwelcome) concealment of (unpalatable) truth

3. They are examples of "(new) technology" / mediums of communication which was/were originally unwanted / (needlessly) frightened people / proved to be non-harmful / beneficial

answers also acceptable which refer to the historical progression showing it is a repeated phenomenon

4. (*a*) They were varied / differing / contrasting / controversial / intense

(*b*) *Word choice:*
  • Comment may be on
  • the varied / contradictory nature of words used:
    NB comment, not mere identification (may be exemplified, e.g. opposing nature of "antagonism" and "enthusiasm")
  • **or** "such" suggesting intensity of reactions
  • **or** "phenomenon" suggests (e.g.) social concern
  • **or** "all at once" suggests disturbing / contradictory nature of reactions

  Structure:
  • comment will be on **list** suggesting multiplicity or **question** being rhetorical or inviting agreement – must be more than mere identification of feature

5. *Any two from:*

Contradiction of "its distinctiveness is not a new phenomenon"	eg (the language) being different is new-fangled/modern/recent
Contradiction of "its use [is] restricted to the young"	eg only children/juveniles/teenagers use it
Contradiction of "it helps rather than hinders literacy"	eg it impedes/restricts/obstructs linguistic/verbal competence
Contradiction of "its long-term impact is negligible"	eg it will have a significant effect
Contradiction of "it is not a disaster"	eg it is a tragedy

6. Just as "hysteria" suggests panic / extremity / irrationality
So the reaction to (innovative) text message language has been excessive / needless / illogical

7. He uses "stories", "reports", "no one was ever able to track down the entire essay"
and "(probably a) hoax", "quoted incessantly"
or
quotation of one of these and comment on its contribution to the sense of untruth and/or credulousness
or
he tells the (apocryphal) essay story / gives an example to show what people were willing to believe

8. Both are acronyms / formed from initial letters / abbreviations.

9. Glosses of **two** of "English has had abbreviated words ever since it began to be written down" – eg this is not new/has a long history
And "attracted criticism" or "complained" – eg have always had a hostile reception/met with disapproval
And "have effectively become new words" – eg have been accepted into the language in their own right

10. They are proof of his point
about literary respectability/long history of deviant forms
or
An assertion that the candidate has no/little idea who these people are
And so this does not help his argument/make anything clear

11. The letters which are used most often (gloss of "frequently occurring")
are not the most easily/most quickly written (gloss of "access" or "input")

12. "Abbreviations" or "(intuitive) response" introduces/points **forward** (to the contractions/reactions covered in the remainder of the paragraph); "technological problem" refers **back** (to the difficulties of entering letters mentioned in the previous paragraph)

13. It signals or introduces a contrast / contributes to a link
Between the practical/technical reasons behind aspects of text language (he has been examining)
And the other (psychological) ones (he goes on to explore)

14. Doubt/disagreement/cynicism/contention/irony/sarcasm

15. Knowledge about/sensitivity to language

16. Answers must relate some aspect of this paragraph to another
feature or idea mentioned or used earlier in the passage

Aspect from last paragraph	*Reference to elsewhere*
Idea of dislike of or bemusement at texting	repeats idea of aversion mentioned in eg opening paragraphs.
Idea of creativity or adaptability	repeats idea of flexibility of language, in eg its not being a new phenomenon.
"There is no disaster pending"	echoes reassurances given elsewhere, eg in "it is not a disaster".
"We will not see a new generation of adults growing up unable to write proper English"/"The language as a whole will not decline"	repeats idea of children's linguistic awareness.
"texting…is language in evolution"	repeats idea of development mentioned elsewhere, eg in adoption of new abbreviated forms.
Upbeat, positive tone of last paragraph	echoes optimistic, affirmative tone throughout the passage (may be exemplified).

ENGLISH INTERMEDIATE 2 CRITICAL ESSAY 2007 TO 2011 EXAMS

Marking Principles for the Critical Essay are as follows:

- The essay should first be read to establish whether the essay achieves success in **all** the Performance Criteria for Grade C, including relevance and the standards for technical accuracy outlined in Note 1 below.
- If minimum standards are not achieved in any **one** or more of the Performance Criteria, the maximum mark which can be awarded is 11.
- If minimum standards have been achieved, then the supplementary marking grids will allow you to place the work on a scale of marks out of 25.
- The Category awarded and the mark should be placed at the end of the essay.

Notes:

1. "Sufficiently accurate" can best be defined in terms of a definition of "consistently accurate".
    - *Consistently accurate*
    A few errors may be present, but these will not be significant in any way. The candidate may use some complex vocabulary and sentence structures. Where appropriate, sentences will show accurate handling of clauses. Linking between sentences will be clear. Paragraphing will reflect a developing line of thought.

    - *Sufficiently accurate*
    As above but with an allowance made for speed and the lack of opportunity to redraft.

2. Using the Category descriptions

    - Categories are not grades. Although derived from performance criteria at C and the indicators of excellence for Grade A, the four categories are designed primarily to assist with placing each candidate response at an appropriate point on a continuum of achievement. Assumptions about final grades or association of final grades with particular categories should not be allowed to influence objective assessment.

    - Once an essay has been deemed to pass the basic criteria, it does not have to meet all the suggestions for Category II (for example) to fall into that Category. More typically there will be a spectrum of strengths and weaknesses which span categories.

GRADE C
Performance Criteria

(a) *Understanding*
As appropriate to task, the response demonstrates understanding of key elements, central concerns and significant details of the text(s).

(b) *Analysis*
The response explains in some detail ways in which aspects of structure/style/language contribute to meaning/effect/impact.

(c) *Evaluation*
The response reveals engagement with the text(s) or aspects of the text(s) and stated or implied evaluation of effectiveness, substantiated by some relevant evidence from the text(s).

(d) *Expression*
Structure, style and language, including use of some appropriate critical terminology, are deployed to communicate meaning clearly and develop a line of thought which is generally relevant to purpose; spelling, grammar and punctuation are sufficiently accurate.

It should be noted that the term "text" encompasses printed, audio or film/video text(s) which may be literary (fiction or non-fiction) or may relate to aspects of media or language.

Language Questions 13 - 15
- The "text" which should be dealt with in a language question is the research which the pupil has done. Examples taken from their research must be there for you to see.
- However, to demonstrate understanding and analysis related to these examples there has to be some ability to generalise from the particular, to classify and comment on what has been discovered. It is not enough merely to produce a list of words in, say, Dundonian with their standard English equivalents. This is merely description and without any further development does not demonstrate understanding of any principle underlying the choice of words.
- The list of features at the head of the section is supportive. A marker would reasonably expect that some such features would be mentioned in the course of the candidate's answer.

Intermediate 2 Critical Essay Supplementary Advice

This advice, which is supplementary to the published Performance Criteria, is designed to assist with the placing of scripts within the full range of marks. However, the Performance Criteria as published give the primary definitions. The mark range for each Category is identified.

IV 8–11	III 12–15	II 16–19	I 20–25
• An essay which falls into this category may do so for a variety of reasons.	**Understanding** • Knowledge of the text(s), and a basic understanding of the **main** concerns will be used .... to provide an answer which is **generally relevant** to the task.	**Understanding** • Knowledge and understanding of the **central** concerns of the text(s) will be used .... to provide an answer which is **mainly relevant** to the task.	**Understanding** • **Secure** knowledge **and some insight** into the central concerns of the text(s) will be demonstrated at this level .... and there will be a line of thought which is **consistently relevant** to the task.
It could be • that it fails to achieve sufficient technical accuracy • or that any knowledge and understanding of the material is not deployed as a response relevant to the task • or that analysis and evaluation attempted are unconvincing • or that the answer is simply too thin.	• Some reference to the text(s) will be made to **support** the candidate's argument.	• Reference to the text(s) will be used as evidence to **promote** the candidate's argument.	• Reference to the text(s) will be used **appropriately** as evidence which helps to **develop** the argument **fully**.
	Analysis • There will be an **explanation** of the contribution of literary/linguistic techniques to the impact of the text(s).	**Analysis** • There will be an **explanation of the effectiveness** of the contribution of literary/linguistic techniques to the impact of the text(s).	**Analysis** • There will be **some insight** shown into the **effectiveness** of the contribution of literary/linguistic techniques to the impact of the text(s).
	Evaluation • There will be **some engagement** with the text(s) which will state or imply an evaluation of its effectiveness.	**Evaluation** • There will be **engagement** with the text(s) which leads to a **generally valid** evaluative stance with respect to the text(s).	**Evaluation** • There will be a **clear engagement** with the text(s) which leads to a **valid** evaluative stance with respect to the material.
	Expression • Language will communicate the argument clearly, and there will be appropriate critical terminology deployed. Spelling, grammar and punctuation will be sufficiently accurate.	**Expression** • Language will communicate the argument **clearly**, and there will be appropriate critical terminology deployed to **aid the argument**. Spelling, grammar and punctuation will be sufficiently accurate.	**Expression** • The language will communicate **effectively** making appropriate use of critical terminology to **further the argument**. Spelling, grammar and punctuation will be sufficiently accurate.

Hey! I've done it

© 2011 SQA/Bright Red Publishing Ltd, All Rights Reserved

Published by Bright Red Publishing Ltd, 6 Stafford Street, Edinburgh, EH3 7AU
Tel: 0131 220 5804, Fax: 0131 220 6710, enquiries: sales@brightredpublishing.co.uk,
www.brightredpublishing.co.uk

Official SQA answers to 978-1-84948-197-7
2007-2011

GLASGOW 5 MARCH 1971 by Edwin Morgan

With a ragged diamond
Of shattered plate-glass
a young man and his girl
are falling backwards into a shop window.
The young man's face
is bristling with fragments of glass
and the girl's leg has caught
on the broken window
and spurts arterial blood
over her wet-look white coat.
Their arms are starfished out
braced for impact,
their faces show surprise, shock,
and the beginning of pain.
The two youths who have pushed them
are about to complete the operation
reaching into the window
to loot what they can smartly.
Their faces show no expression.
It is a sharp clear night
in Sauchiehall Street.
In the background two drivers
keep their eyes on the road.

GLASGOW 5 MARCH 1971 by Edwin Morgan

With a ragged diamond
Of shattered plate-glass
a young man and his girl
are falling backwards into a shop window.
The young man's face
is bristling with fragments of glass
and the girl's leg has caught
on the broken window
and spurts arterial blood
over her wet-look white coat.
Their arms are starfished out
braced for impact,
their faces show surprise, shock,
and the beginning of pain.
The two youths who have pushed them
are about to complete the operation
reaching into the window
to loot what they can smartly.
Their faces show no expression.
It is a sharp clear night
in Sauchiehall Street.
In the background two drivers
keep their eyes on the road.